My Family

Sheila Kinkade

Photographs by Elaine Little

Indonesia

Belgium

Foreword by Kathleen Kennedy Townsend

A GLOBAL FUND FOR
Children
BOOK

 Charlesbridge

Foreword

Families can be both wonderful and a challenge. I am the mother of four wonderful daughters, the eldest of eleven brothers and sisters, the aunt of over thirty nieces and nephews, and I have about seventy cousins—many of whom have children of their own.

One of the most rewarding experiences people all around the world share is being part of a family. Each family is special and different. Some children are blessed to have big extended families with loving grandparents and lots of cousins, while others have small families. Some have moms and dads at home while other kids have special relationships with uncles and aunts, siblings, grandparents, stepmoms, or stepdads. Quite often, friends are a big part of a family and can be just like parents or aunts or uncles. At the heart of any family are the love and the care family members show each other every day.

Our families are our first teachers. My parents, grandparents, aunts, and uncles taught me many important lessons that I have passed along to my four daughters. One of those is the value of service and having the courage and the faith to make a real difference in other people's lives, both inside and outside of your family.

While family life can be full of laughter, joy, and play, all families face challenges and tough times. The true test of a family is how well its members support one another during times of both joy and sadness. At their best, families give you a strong sense of your roots, and the wings with which to fly and to realize your dreams.

My father, Senator Robert F. Kennedy, said: "The future is not a gift: it is an achievement. Every generation helps make its own future." With this in mind, I wish a bright future for all young people who read this book. As you shape your own lives, may you shape the lives of others. And, always know that standing beside you is the love and encouragement of a supportive family.

The Honorable Kathleen Kennedy Townsend
Former Lt. Governor, State of Maryland

Bangladesh

Do you know what a family is?

A family is people with whom you belong, people who love you. Families come in many different shapes and sizes. Families are made up of parents and children, sisters and brothers, cousins, aunts and uncles, and grandparents. Some are big, with many children and lots of relatives. Others are small, with only one parent and a child. Sometimes people adopt children who have no one to care for them and welcome them into their own family.

Philippines

Slovakia

Portugal

Zambia

Most children around the world grow up feeling safe and valued through the love they receive from their family. A baby in Zambia feels loved when his mother carries him with her to the market. A child in the Philippines feels cared for when he gets a bath. No matter where a child lives, a hug or a kiss says, "I love you."

Greece

Family members show their love for each other in many ways

Philippines

United States

Brazil

and care for one another.

As children grow up, they receive special care from their parents, grandparents, older siblings, and in some cases, the extended family or community. Caring for a child means listening and responding to their needs. When a child is sick or sad, there's no better place to be than with family. Sometimes all it takes is a warm hug to make a child feel better.

Mexico

United States

Poland

United States

Philippines

United Kingdom

Jordan

Families live together . . .

Brazil

Parents and children share many experiences at home—talking, eating, reading, playing, and sleeping. Every home is different and reflects a family's traditions and way of life. Families live in homes of all sizes and shapes. Many families around the world live simply with few possessions, while others combine their workplace and their living space.

United States

Bangladesh

in many different types of homes.

Philippines

Italy

Zambia

While many children grow up in rural villages and small towns, more and more children live in cities. On the island of Sicily, in Italy, many families live in brightly colored houses right next to each other. In some remote villages in Zambia, children live in round huts made of mud and dried grass. And in the Philippines, some children live in houses built over the water.

Ecuador

Switzerland

Families have fun and play together,

No matter where they live, children laugh, leap, clap, shout, and play. Playing can mean getting your face painted or feeding pigeons in a busy city square. It can mean taking a ride at an amusement park or hitting a volleyball over the net. Playing often involves learning something new, like how to catch a ball or play a new game.

United States

Germany

Japan

Egypt

Jordan

eat together,

At mealtimes family members come together to enjoy good food and one another's company. Families often tell stories and talk about their day while sharing a meal together. Depending on where they live, families eat different types of food. Three brothers in Morocco share couscous. In Slovakia, a family enjoys an apple pastry for dessert.

Slovakia

Morocco

United States

Philippines

Israel

and enjoy going places.

Families often walk or drive places together. Going places can mean walking to school or doing simple errands like buying food. Or, it can mean going on a trip or attending a special event, such as a fair or a sports competition. Sometimes it even means going on an adventure such as a camel ride in the desert.

Australia

Egypt

United States

Slovakia

South Africa

Family members teach and learn from one another,

Parents teach young children how to walk, talk, read, and count. They also teach what is right and wrong. Grandparents, brothers, and sisters are also teachers. A father helps his son ring a bell, while a sister introduces her brother to a rabbit. Family members offer encouragement so that children feel comfortable exploring new activities like ice-skating.

Sweden

India

Japan

work together,

Children help their parents with simple tasks like cleaning their homes. Sometimes, both parents and children volunteer to assist other families who are building or repairing their homes. In many parts of the world, children help their family earn money through farming or fishing. Others help their parents sell vegetables and crafts. A father and son go fishing together in Morocco. In Jordan, a family offers camel and donkey rides to tourists.

Philippines

Jordan

United States

Morocco

and worship and pray together.

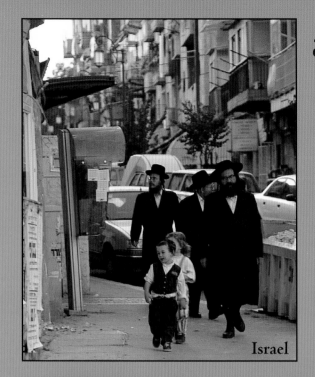
Israel

From a very early age, many children join their family in worship and prayer. A family's religious practices depend on the family's beliefs. Some are Christian, some are Muslim, some are Jewish, some are Hindu, and some are Buddhist. Still other families follow other religions or have other beliefs. But all over the world, you will find prayer, faith, and shared values an important part of family life.

Slovakia

Thailand

Philippines

Russia

Special moments and experiences within a family are remembered for a lifetime. One of the ways families collect memories is through photographs. Families take photos when they go to new places and during special celebrations, like birthdays, weddings, and holidays. Families also save important items, like clothing or jewelry, to pass down to their children.

United States

Families cherish memories of the experiences they share.

Zambia

United States

Cowan Family Reunion

Slovakia

And while every family is different, they are all part of the human family.

Philippines

United States

No matter where they live, families care for others in their community. Children reach out to other children who need help or are simply looking for a friend. Sometimes just a smile or an outstretched hand is all you need to connect to someone. In today's world, it's important to remember that, in addition to our own family, we are also part of a bigger human family. We depend on each other every day to help make sure the world is a good home for all families.

Egypt

Kenya

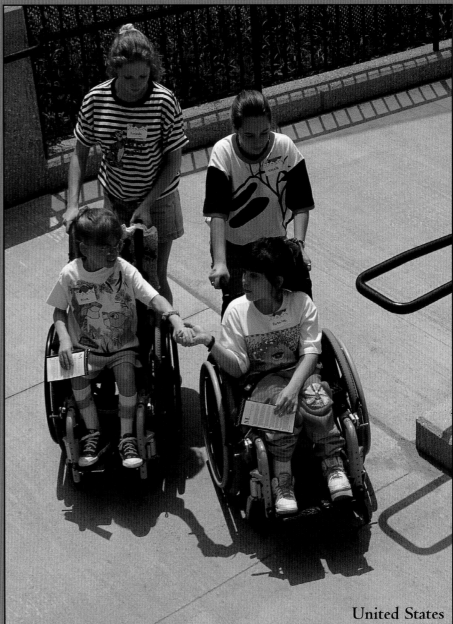
United States

New Zealand

Ecuador

Zimbabwe

United States

Mexico

Ecuador

Brazil

To my mother for her love and support—S. K.

To my wonderful husband and daughter,
    Rick and Sarah—E. L.

Bangladesh

My Family was developed by the Global Fund for Children (www.globalfundforchildren.org), a nonprofit organization committed to advancing the dignity of children and youth around the world. Global Fund for Children books teach young people to value diversity and help them become productive and caring global citizens.

The support of *My Family* has been provided by the Flora Family Foundation and the Virginia Wellington Cabot Foundation.

Developed by Global Fund for Children Books
1101 Fourteenth Street, NW, Suite 420
Washington, DC 20005
(202) 331-9003 • www.globalfundforchildren.org

Published by Charlesbridge
85 Main Street
Watertown, MA 02472
(617) 926-0329
www.charlesbridge.com

Details about the donation of royalties can be obtained by writing to Charlesbridge and the Global Fund for Children.

Library of Congress Cataloging-in-Publication Data
Kinkade, Sheila, 1962–
    My family / Sheila Kinkade ; photographs by Elaine Little.
      p. cm.
    ISBN-13: 978-1-57091-662-5; ISBN-10: 1-57091-662-4 (reinforced for library use)
    ISBN-13: 978-1-57091-691-5; ISBN-10: 1-57091-691-8 (softcover)
1. Family—Juvenile literature. 2. Family—Cross-cultural studies—Juvenile literature.
I. Little, Elaine, 1958– II. Title.
HQ744.K56 2006
306.85—dc22   2005005888

Printed in Thailand
(hc) 10 9 8 7 6 5 4 3 2
(sc) 10 9 8 7 6 5 4 3 2

Color separations by Chroma Graphics, Singapore
Printed and bound by Imago
Production supervision by Brian G. Walker